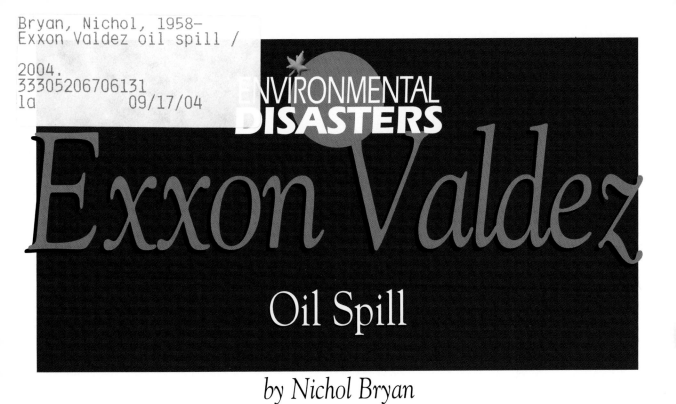

ENVIRONMENTAL DISASTERS

Exxon Valdez

Oil Spill

by Nichol Bryan

Please visit our web site at: www.worldalmanaclibrary.com
For a free color catalog describing World Almanac® Library's list of high-quality books and multimedia programs, call 1-800-848-2928 (USA) or 1-800-387-3178 (Canada). World Almanac® Library's fax: (414) 332-3567.

Library of Congress Cataloging-in-Publication Data

Bryan, Nichol, 1958-
    Exxon Valdez: oil spill / by Nichol Bryan.
      p. cm. — (Environmental disasters)
    Summary: Describes the oil tanker Exxon Valdez, the events that led up to its disastrous oil spill in 1989, and the effects of the spill on the Alaskan environment.
    Includes bibliographical references and index.
    ISBN 0–8368–5506–X (lib. bdg.)
    ISBN 0–8368–5513–2 (softcover)
    1. Oil spills—Environmental aspects—Alaska—Prince William Sound Region—Juvenile literature. 2. Tankers—Accidents—Environmental aspects—Alaska—Prince William Sound Region—Juvenile literature. 3. Exxon Valdez (Ship)—Juvenile literature. [1. Oil spills—Alaska—Prince William Sound region. 2. Tankers—Accidents. 3. Exxon Valdez (Ship).] I. Title. II. Environmental disasters (Milwaukee, Wis.)
    TD427.P4B79   2003
    363.738'2'097983—dc21   2003047991

First published in 2004 by
World Almanac® Library
330 West Olive Street, Suite 100
Milwaukee, WI 53212 USA

Copyright © 2004 by World Almanac® Library.

Produced by Lownik Communication Services
Cover design and page production: Heidi Bittner-Zastrow
Picture researcher: Jean Lownik
World Almanac® Library art direction: Tammy Gruenewald
World Almanac® Library series editor: Carol Ryback

Photo Credits: Cover, © Greenpeace/Visser; 4, Heidi Bittner-Zastrow; 5, 7, 23, 24(b), 28, © Greenpeace/Merjenburgh; 6, 8, 9(b), 12, 14, 16, 17, 18, 19(b), 20, 21, 24(t), 25, 26, 29(b), 30, 31, 33, 35(b), 38(b), 40, 43, Natalie B. Fobes; 9(t), © REUTERS Kevin Lamarque © Reuters NewMedia Inc./CORBIS; 10, 19(t), 29(t), 32, © Exxon Valdez Oil Spill Trust Council, National Oceanic and Atmospheric Administration (NOAA); 11, © Terry W. Eggers/CORBIS; 13, © Danny Lehman/CORBIS; 22, © AFP/CORBIS; 27, 35(t), 36, © Reuters; 34, © Gary Braasch/CORBIS; 37, AFP PHOTO AL GRILLO © AFP/CORBIS; 38, Anchorage Daily News (map); 39, © Bettmann/CORBIS; 41, REUTERS Miguel Vidal © Reuters NewMedia Inc./CORBIS

Printed in the United States of America

1 2 3 4 5 6 7 8 9 07 06 05 04 03

Cover: Two years after the 1989 *Exxon Valdez* oil spill, the hands of a Greenpeace volunteer became covered in oil while surveying Diesel Beach on Knight Island in Prince William Sound.

Contents

Introduction
The Day the Water Died 5

Chapter 1
Power from the Wilderness 10

Chapter 2
Black Waves of Oil 16

Chapter 3
Saving Paradise 23

Chapter 4
"A Part of Us Is Missing" 34

Time Line 44

Glossary 45

For More Information/Web Sites 46

Index 47-48

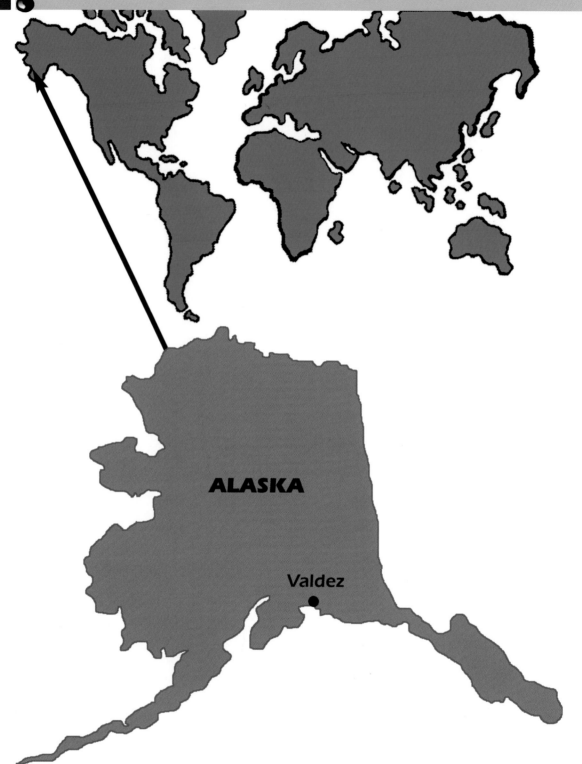

ALASKA

Valdez

Introduction

The Day The
Water Died

It was midnight on the quiet waters of Prince William Sound. In the seaport town of Valdez (val DEEZ), Alaska, and in the Native Alaskan villages up and down the coast, most people were asleep. The shores of the beaches and islands — crowded with seals, otters, and seabirds — seemed peaceful. A wet snow fell silently on land and sea.

But just off the coast, a giant ship was sailing blindly toward disaster.

The oil supertanker, *Exxon Valdez*, had wandered far off course. Just after midnight, on March 24, 1989, the ship rammed into rocky Bligh Reef. The impact ripped a hole in the steel hull.

More than two hundred sixty thousand barrels of crude oil — about

The supertanker *Exxon Valdez* sits hard aground Bligh Reef but does not show any damage in this photo taken after the oil spill in Prince William Sound, Alaska.

A mother harbor seal nuzzles her pup. Oil totally covers both animals. Biologists believe that the oil spill killed most of the newborn pups.

11 million gallons (42 million liters) — started gushing into the pristine waters of the Sound.

It was the largest oil spill in U.S. history. And it happened in the worst possible place — a remote environment, rich in diversity and wildlife, and far from emergency cleanup equipment.

The *Exxon Valdez* spill also turned into the biggest environmental disaster in American history. The spill soiled hundreds of miles of Alaskan coastline with thick gobs of crude oil. The cleanup cost more than $2 billion and required ten thousand people using one thousand boats and one hundred planes and

"We're Gonna Be Here for a While"
"You should have us on your radar. We've fetched up, ah, hard aground, north of Goose Island, off Bligh Reef and, ah, evidently leaking some oil and we're gonna be here for a while."

— Joseph Hazelwood, captain of the *Exxon Valdez*, radioing the U.S. Coast Guard about the accident

Oil floats on the water surrounding the *Exxon Valdez* (left) and the ship sent to assist in the crisis.

helicopters. Thousands of volunteers rushed to the area to try to save wildlife. Even so, the oil killed hundreds of thousands of seabirds, otters, harbor seals, bald eagles, and killer whales. Billions of salmon and herring eggs were destroyed by the poison slick.

No human lives were lost in the disaster. But the impact of the spill on the people who lived and worked in the Sound was great. Fishermen who depended on the rich harvest from the area were told it was off-limits to commercial fishing. Even worse, the Native Alaskan people who relied on the sea for their very existence were suddenly without a source of food. The everyday lives of these Native people were totally disrupted by the spill — and by the flood of cleanup and rescue workers who suddenly

"Killing the Water"
"The excitement of the [fishing] season had just begun, and then, we heard the news, oil in the water, lots of oil killing lots of water. It is too shocking to understand. Never in the millennium of our tradition have we thought it possible for the water to die, but it is true."
— Chief Walter Meganack, Alaskan Native

mobbed their beaches.

It took years to clean up the mess left by the *Exxon Valdez*. Even more years passed before the animal populations in the Sound recovered from the damage. Fifteen years after the accident, buried pockets of oil

An animal rescue team took this oil-covered sea otter to a rehabilitation center after the spill, hoping to save its life.

still contaminate the area's shores. Even now, the populations of some native animal species remain lower than their pre-spill numbers.

The Energy Debate

The *Exxon Valdez* spill not only affected Alaska's people and animals, but also the United States as a whole. People across the country reacted with outrage that the Alaskan wilderness had been fouled. They watched in alarm as television reports showed pictures of dying otters and seabirds. They demanded to know who was responsible.

And they told their lawmakers to ensure it didn't happen again. Environmental damage from the *Exxon Valdez* accident was much greater than that caused by the slight radiation leak in 1979 from the Three Mile Island nuclear power plant in Middletown, Pennsylvania.

But the causes of the *Exxon* spill, and the solutions to future pollution of the Arctic, aren't as simple as they might seem. Before it ran aground, the *Exxon Valdez* was playing its part in a national energy policy. That policy called for the United States to cut back on its use of oil from other countries. After the energy crisis of the 1970s, people wanted the government to make sure that foreign countries could never again threaten the nation's oil supply. In response, Congress cleared the way for increased oil production in Alaska. The *Exxon Valdez* — like hundreds of other similar tanker ships — were part of the U.S. effort to win its energy independence.

Much of that history was forgotten after the spill. Instead, people called for more protection for Alaskan waterways

Young protesters oppose a clear-cutting operation near Cordova, Alaska. The movement to protect Alaska's environmentally sensitive areas gained renewed strength after the *Exxon Valdez* spill.

and other environmentally sensitive areas. Public support for oil exploration and drilling of the U.S. coasts dropped. The production of oil in the United States slowed down, even though its use of oil grew. Imports of foreign oil increased. In 1991 and again in 2003, the U.S. waged war in the Middle East. Some critics of the government said those wars were about control of that region's oil.

A decade and a half after the *Exxon Valdez* oil spill, the argument about oil, energy, and the environment continues. Instead of pushing for conservation of resources, President George W. Bush —

who took office in early 2001 — urged lawmakers to expand oil exploration and drilling in the United States, including areas of Alaska that used to be off-limits to oil companies. Bush's plan caused a storm of protest from environmental activists and others who remember the damage caused by the *Exxon Valdez*.

But the United States's appetite for oil continues to grow. Americans are faced with the choice of developing alternative energy technologies that cut their dependency on oil or accepting the possibly negative environmental and military consequences of refusing to cut oil consumption.

Citizens in the United States seem hopelessly stuck in this endless energy debate. Like the *Exxon Valdez*, they are "hard aground."

"Something Sacred Had Been Defiled."
"The most important loss for many who will never visit Prince William Sound was the aesthetic sense that something sacred in the relatively unspoiled land and waters of Alaska had been defiled."
— From the final report of the Alaska Oil Spill Commission

Chapter 1

Power from the **Wilderness**

Clean. Untouched. Wild. These are the words that come to mind at the mention of Alaska's Prince William Sound. Its clear, icy waters team with otters and seals. Pink salmon splash their way up from the Sound into rivers and streams to breed. Thousands of kittiwakes and other arctic birds circle and wheel around cliff-side rookeries. Pods of killer whales break the surface hunting for schools of herring The Sound is also a harsh, unforgiving place.

For months in the winter, the Sun barely rises. Glaciers spawn huge, blue-green icebergs that bob in the frigid water. Temperatures can drop below -20 degrees Fahrenheit (-30 degrees Celsius).

But this very harshness helped keep Prince William Sound clean and wild.

An orca, or killer whale, breeches in Prince William Sound.

A mountain backdrop frames the skyline of Anchorage — Alaska's largest city. Anchorage is the starting point of the Iditarod Trail Sled Dog Race. The annual event runs 1,150 miles (1,850 km) between Anchorage and Nome, Alaska, and is often called "The Last Great Race on Earth."

Only the hardiest humans — the Native Alaskans, fishermen, and mineral prospectors — called Alaska home. That's why Alaska, the largest U.S. state, is also the least populated. With just one person per square mile, humans exert little pressure on animal habitats. In 2000, only three cities in all of Alaska had populations of more than 30,000 people. They were Anchorage (pop. 260,000), Juneau (pop. 30,700), and Fairbanks (pop. 30,200).

Prince William Sound is a massive waterway bounded by more than 2,000 miles (3,200 km) of shoreline dotted with islands. Its vast network of bays, inlets, and glaciers open into the Gulf of Alaska. The Sound is surrounded by mountains and forests, which are an

Bigger and Bigger Tankers

Since the end of World War II, oil tankers have gotten bigger and bigger. Before the 1950s, a tanker weighing 30,000 tons (27,200 tonnes) was considered big. In order to meet the growing demand for oil, companies began building so-called supertankers. Very Large Crude Carriers (VLCCs) weigh up to 270,000 tons (244,940 tonnes) and Ultra Large Crude Carriers (ULCCS) can weight up to 400,000 tons (362,874 tonnes).

The *Exxon Valdez* was a VLCC. It was one of the largest ships to serve the port of Valdez and measured 967 feet (295 m) long and 166 feet (51 meters) wide — the length of three football fields. The *Valdez* was designed to carry more than 50 million gallons (190 million l) of oil.

Oil and the Alaskan Economy

Oil has been the lifeblood of Alaska's economy since the discovery of the Prudhoe Bay oil fields in 1968. Oil-drilling and related operations bring in $8 billion to the state every year. The Alaskan government gets more than eighty percent of its funding from oil revenues. In fact, Alaska abolished its income and sales taxes thanks to oil and instead established the Alaska Permanent Fund, which gives every eligible Alaskan resident an annual check from the oil profits. In 2002, that amount was about $1,500.

ideal home for birds and mammals. The abundant wildlife in the Sound includes fish such as salmon and herring, shellfish such as crab and shrimp, and marine mammals such as whales, sea lions, seals, and otters. Thousands of birds, including eagles, trumpeter swans, ducks, and geese live there. Bears, moose, deer, wolves, and other land animals thrive along the Sound's diverse shoreline.

The rich resources of Prince William Sound have drawn human settlers since prehistoric times. Native groups such as Inuits (Eskimos) and Aleuts have lived in the area since their ancestors are believed to have crossed a land mass from Asia thousands of years ago.

Russians were the first European settlers in the area in the early 1800s.

Five years after the oil spill, Gail Evandoff, the leader of the Aleut village of Chenega, still found oil on nearby beaches. The spill destroyed the Aleut's subsistence lifestyle.

They were followed by American settlers in 1867, the year the United States bought the land from Russia. Alaska achieved U.S. statehood in 1959.

Oil Changes Alaska

For much of its history, the residents of Alaska made their living fishing, trapping, or gold mining. That began to change with the discovery of oil near the end of the 1800s. According to legend, in 1896 bear hunter Tom White slipped and fell into a slimy black pool near the mouth of the Copper River. Back at his cabin, he wiped himself down. When he threw the slimy cleanup rags into the fireplace, they burst into huge flames. Curious, White went back to the black pool and threw in a match. According to the story, the pool burned for a week.

Whatever the truth of Tom White's tale, oil drilling in Alaska started on a small scale in 1902. Production increased when large oil fields were

In the late 1980s, about 8.5 million gallons (33 million l) of oil a day flowed through the 800-mile (1,300-km) Trans-Alaska Pipeline System that crosses Alaska's environmentally sensitive landscape. At present, oil flows at about half that volume.

discovered on the southern Kenai Peninsula, south of Anchorage, in 1957. Soon thousands of oil-industry workers flooded into Alaska from the lower forty-eight states.

In 1968, one of the largest deposits of oil in North America was discovered in Prudhoe Bay on Alaska's north coast. Surveyors estimated that the field would produce almost ten billion barrels of oil. But drilling there posed problems. The treacherous Beaufort Sea was too rough for shipping, even when it wasn't blocked by ice. Oil producers needed a way to transport their product to the refineries.

Seven major oil companies found a solution. They formed a group called Alyeska (al ee EHS kah), after the Alaskan Native word meaning "mainland." The group proposed building a pipeline that would carry oil across Alaska from Prudhoe Bay on the northern coast to the ice-free port of Valdez on the southern coast — a distance of 800 miles (1,300 km).

Environmentalists opposed the plan. They thought the massive structure would harm animal populations. But when tensions in the Middle East prompted an oil shortage in the U.S., Alyeska got permission to begin building the pipeline in 1973. Four years and almost $8 billion later, oil began to flow through the Trans-Alaska Pipeline System (TAPS).

Oil loaded into tankers in Valdez was shipped to refineries along the West Coast. The tanker traffic increased

"No Significant Damage"

"I am satisfied that tanker traffic to and from Port Valdez, and operation of an oil port there will not cause any significant damage to the marine environment or to fisheries interests."

—L. R. Beyon, Alyeska environmental expert, speaking in 1971

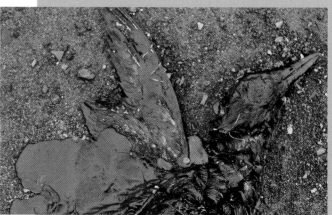

steadily. During the twelve years between the opening of TAPS and the *Exxon Valdez* spill, tankers from Valdez had passed through Price William Sound more than 8,700 times with no serious accidents. In 2003, TAPS tankers transported about eighteen percent of the oil used by the United States.

The American Hunger for Oil

The United States' appetite for oil drives oil tanker traffic in the Sound. Throughout the twentieth century, the nation's industries grew quickly and a growing population demanded millions of new cars and trucks. Other products made from oil — such as plastics and fertilizers — were being made in record quantities. All this growth meant that Americans needed more and more oil. By 1980, the average U.S. citizen was using more than thirty-one barrels — 1,300 gallons (4,921 liters) of oil — every year. Each oil barrel holds 42 gallons (159 l). That oil came from all over the globe — from oil fields in Alaska and the Middle East, as well as from wells drilled in the continental United States.

Moving so much oil around was risky business. As larger numbers of bigger tankers roamed the seas, the chance that they would run into reefs — or into each other — grew. In 1976, the tanker *Argo*

Merchant ran aground off Nantucket Island, Massachusetts, spilling more than 7.7 million gallons (29 million l) of oil. Two years later, the *Amoco Cadiz* polluted 125 miles (200 km) of French coastline when it ran aground and spilled around 67 million gallons (250 million l) of crude oil.

Accidents like these roused public opinion and led to calls for safer oil shipping. Oil-shipping nations agreed to safety regulations and minimum construction requirements for oil tankers. The regulations made tankers safer and reduced the frequency of oil spills.

To win approval for the TAPS, Alyeska also had to promise to follow strict safety regulations. These rules controlled how many tankers could run in and out of Prince William Sound. They also controlled the size and work schedules of the crews that operated the tankers and spelled out how tankers would operate.

As the years wore on, the tankers serving the port of Valdez remained accident free. Tanker traffic became routine. As experts would later point out, Alyeska started to loosen up on its safety regulations. The operators were convinced that oil shipments were safe and there was no need to worry.

In 1989, that sense of safety was forever shattered.

The energy crisis of the 1970s

In 1973, the Arab oil-producing states decided to reduce their oil output as a way to punish the United States for its support of Israel. The result was skyrocketing prices for gasoline and home heating oil in the United States. Long lines formed at gas pumps as people tried to "top off" their tanks, fearing gas shortages.

This energy crisis made many Americans demand that the U.S. government take steps to cut the dependence on foreign oil. It led to the construction of the Trans-Alaska Pipeline System. The crisis also forced lawmakers to support the development and use of alternative energy sources, such as solar and wind power.

Chapter 2

Black Waves of Oil

For most of the crew of the *Exxon Valdez*, Thursday, March 23, 1989, was a busy day.

The big tanker put into the Alyeska Marine Terminal near the town of Valdez the day before to take on a load of oil.

Ship and terminal crews didn't waste time. Before dawn on Thursday morning, the ship began to load its cargo. One hundred thousand barrels of crude oil an hour were pumped into the *Exxon Valdez*'s hold.

For some of the crew's officers, oil-

Oil continued leaking from the *Exxon Valdez* while it was stranded on Bligh Reef. Tugboats stand by, waiting to assist the hapless tanker.

loading time presented a chance to go ashore before the tanker pushed off again that night. The ship's captain, Joseph Hazelwood, left that morning for the nearby town of Valdez. While in port, Hazelwood took care of ship's business and did a little shopping. While waiting for a pizza to take back to the ship that evening, he also drank some vodka. As captain of the *Exxon Valdez*, Hazelwood should not have been drinking any alcoholic beverages.

Last-Minute Safety Checks

The *Exxon Valdez* was loaded and ready to depart by the time Hazelwood and his officers got back that evening at about 8:30 P.M. The crew performed last-minute safety checks. Just after 9:00 P.M. its lines were cast off, and two tugboats began to haul the supertanker away

from the dock. By 9:35 P.M., the ship had left the Valdez harbor. Hazelwood left his command center — called the bridge — even though Exxon's rules required two ship's officers on duty as oil tankers passed through the narrow harbor entrance. Marine pilot William Murphy was left in charge.

At 10:49 P.M., the tanker was through the Valdez Narrows. Murphy's job was finished, so he disembarked the

"The Inevitable Mistakes of Human Beings"

"Hazelwood's activities in town that day and on the ship that night would become a key focus of accident inquiries, the cause of a state criminal prosecution, and the basis of widespread media sensation. Without intending to minimize the impact of Hazelwood's actions, however, one basic conclusion of this report is that the grounding at Bligh Reef represents much more than the error of a possibly drunken skipper: It was the result of the gradual degradation of oversight and safety practices that had been intended, twelve years before, to safeguard and backstop the inevitable mistakes of human beings."

— From the Final Report of the Alaska Oil Spill Commission

suptertanker and went aboard one of the tugboats to go back to the mainland. Hazelwood took command of the bridge and increased the ship's speed.

To avoid collisions, shipping authorities have declared two "lanes" through Prince William Sound. Ships leaving the Sound use the west lane, and tankers heading to Valdez stay to the east. When necessary, ships can switch lanes to avoid icebergs. Hazelwood did just that, asking for permission to shift to the inbound lane. The Valdez Vessel Traffic Center gave the okay.

A Way through the Ice

At 11:30 P.M., Hazelwood told the traffic center he was heading even further east, to "wind my way through the ice." He also said he was reducing speed for the tricky maneuver, although records show the *Exxon Valdez* continued to speed up. The captain then set another new course down the inbound lane — without informing the Valdez Vessel Traffic Center of this move — before putting the supertanker on automatic pilot.

The *Exxon Valdez* continued to drift east, past the incoming-lane boundaries, into dangerous waters. Hazelwood apparently never noticed the problem. Shortly before midnight, he gave his final orders about steering the tanker back into the outbound lane and left the bridge again — another violation of company rules. Third Mate Gregory Cousins was alone on the bridge

Cousins began to move the big tanker back to the outbound lanes. Suddenly a lookout called to him with alarming news. The light marking Bligh

Ships must move carefully through the iceberg-filled waters of Prince William Sound.

"You Can Just Smell the Death"
"A lot of people from Cordova might have bad attitudes, because they're seeing their lifestyle go down the drain. They say, 'You're from Cordova, you have a bad attitude.' But I've lost my way of life . . . You can just smell the death coming out of the sea."

— Devan Ruel,
a fisherman from Cordova, Alaska

Reef, which should have been off the left (port) side of the ship, was actually on the right (starboard) side of the ship. The *Exxon Valdez* was on a collision course with a huge underwater rock wall.

Third Mate Cousins tried to change course, but the loaded, 295,000-ton (267,000-tonne) ship, already near its maximum speed, was slow to turn. The ship was approaching the reef very quickly. Cousins called Hazelwood to warn him of the danger. The two men were on the phone when the crew felt six sharp jolts through the hull of the ship. They were on the reef.

When the *Exxon Valdez* struck Bligh Reef, it ripped open eight of its eleven cargo tanks. Tons of oil spilled into the Sound so quickly they formed waves of oil 3 feet (1 m) high. In the first three hours, 6 million gallons (23 million l) of oil gushed out of the damaged tanker.

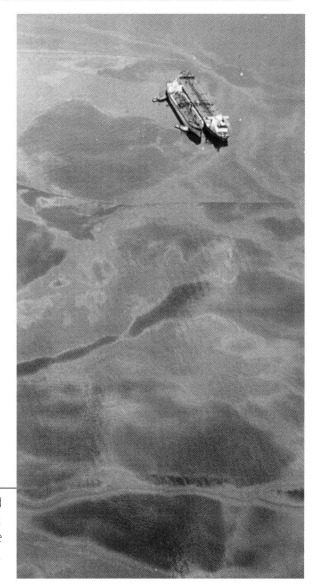

Oil floats on the surface of Prince William Sound shortly after the accident. Five years later, oil was still found just below the surface of beaches in the Sound.

"I Feared For My Life"

"The vessel began to shudder, and that woke me. As a chief officer, you kind of learn to sleep lightly, anyway. Then, I heard a clank, clank, clank, and I knew something was wrong. . . . I knew right then that my life would never be the same again. And, I don't mind telling you that I feared for my life, wondered if I'd ever see my wife again."

— Testimony of *Exxon Valdez* Chief Mate James Kunkel
before the National Traffic Safety Board

Hazelwood rushed back to the bridge after he felt the shocks. For fifteen minutes he tried to free the tanker from the reef, engines going full-throttle. Then he shut down the engines, ordered his chief mate to inspect the damage, and radioed the Coast Guard about the ship's grounding.

At 12:30 A.M., Chief Mate James Kunkel returned with bad news. He told Captain Hazelwood that the ship's cargo tanks had ruptured and said Hazelwood should not try to move the ship again. Hazelwood told the officer to go back and learn more about the damage. Then the captain ordered the ships engines to full speed again and tried once more to

get the *Exxon Valdez* off the rocks. He kept on trying for more than an hour. At 1:41 A.M. that Friday — Good Friday, 1989 — Captain Joseph Hazelwood finally admitted defeat.

Hazelwood's call to the Coast Guard set off a chain reaction of phone calls to Exxon headquarters and around the world, as company officials tried to find emergency equipment to fight the spill. According to Alyeska's spill response plan, spill response equipment was supposed to be at the scene within five hours. But very little oil-containment equipment was ready at Valdez.

Officials had to bring in equipment from much farther away. It was nearly

Oil that spilled from the *Exxon Valdez* covered rocks in Prince William Sound.

Rescue efforts proved useless for this oil-covered pigeon guillemot.

ten hours before the cleanup crews arrived at the scene. By this time, the thick, greasy, black oil slick had already spread for miles around.

How Oil Spreads

Crude oil is actually a mix of many different chemicals. When it spills into the ocean, it breaks down into separate parts, each of which behaves in a different way. The lighter parts of the oil evaporate. The heavier parts mix with surrounding water to form a sticky mixture called "mousse." This eventually sinks to the bottom or washes up on shore, forming a thick, tar-like mass that ruins the habitats of sea and shore creatures alike.

Floating oil hurts animals in many ways. Oil makes fur and feathers sticky, forcing out the air that keeps the animals warm. In this way, oil makes birds and mammals freeze to death. When animals try to lick off the oil — or if one animal eats another oil-covered animal — they take in poisons that can make them sick or kill them.

Oil hurts fish primarily by killing the eggs they lay. Oil gets inside fish when they eat oil-covered plants or smaller organisms. The fish then store up oily toxins in their livers and other body tissues, causing disease in the fish and making the fish themselves toxic. Eagles, bears, other fish-eating creatures, and humans wind up getting poisoned, too, as the oil works its way up the food chain.

Residents of Prince William Sound reacted with shock and fear when they heard about the spill. Commercial fishermen wondered how the spill would affect their livelihood. For Native

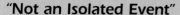

"Not an Isolated Event"

"The *Exxon Valdez* disaster was not an isolated event. It was just one in a series of ongoing major oil spills, from tankers and other sources, that have wreaked environmental havoc across the world. . . . The only way truly to insure that tragedies such as the *Exxon Valdez* are not repeated is for the industrialized world to wean itself from its dependence on fossil fuels."

— Statement from the
environmental group Greenpeace

Alaskans living along the shore, the news was even more frightening. The stranded tanker ran aground just a few miles from the village of Tatitlek. Residents there could smell the evaporating oil fumes for days afterwards. People in Tatitlek were afraid that everything they ate would be poisoned.

As one Native villager put it, "This is hurting more than anything else we ever experienced. It's like losing everything you had."

On November 13, 2002, the hull of the oil tanker *Prestige* cracked during a storm off the northwest coast of Spain. It was towed farther out to sea to help prevent its cargo — more than 20 million gallons (76 million l) of crude oil — from reaching land. At least 5 million gallons (18 million l) of oil that spilled from the ship fouled Spain's coastline. About one week later, the tanker broke in two and sank with most of its oil still in the hold. The *Prestige* now sits 130 nautical miles (210 km) from shore and 2 miles (3.5 km) under the surface. Salvage workers hope to remove some of the oil.

By contrast, the *Exxon Valdez* did not sink when it hit Bligh Reef. But the *Exxon Valdez* spilled twice as much oil in an area that is not as easily flushed by natural wind and wave action — which increased the impact of the spill.

Chapter 3

Saving
Paradise

Exxon immediately took control of the cleanup efforts after the size of the *Exxon Valdez* disaster became clear. Its first goal was to clean up as much of the spreading oil slick as possible before it washed ashore. Once the oil reached shallow waters and beaches, damage to wildlife would mount quickly.

First, cleanup workers tried to burn the oil off the water. This is often the fastest way to clean up an oil spill. Crews hauled the oil slick away from the damaged tanker. They floated a long flexible rod — called a boom — between two ships as they moved slowly through

Early cleanup crews used high-powered hot-water jets after the oil spill. Unfortunately, high temperatures cooked some sea creatures the cleanup effort meant to save.

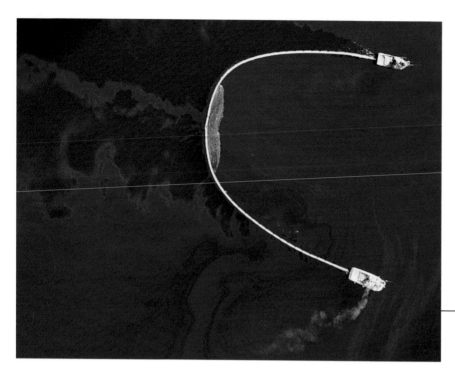

Fishermen deploy a boom in an attempt to keep oil away from millions of fry in a fish hatchery.

the slick. Once the boom had captured enough oil off the surface, they set it afire. This technique worked at first. But high winds, rough seas, and rain kept the workers from burning very much oil. The bad weather also helped push the oil further into Prince William Sound.

Exxon workers also tried to use skimmers to clean up the spill. Skimmers are devices that suck the oil off the surface of the water, after it's been collected in a boom. It took more than one day for the skimmers to reach Prince William Sound and the area of the spill. As the crews began working, thick oil mixed with heavy floating seaweed and clogged the skimmers. Every clog meant hours of delay while the skimmers were repaired. Bad weather also kept the skimmers from reaching the oil slick.

Cleanup crews hoped to use one final method to attack the slick before it washed ashore. Low-flying aircraft can spray chemicals called dispersants

"We Try to Save Just a Few."

"With many hundreds of otters dying, we try to save just a few, and most of them, we're not successful, and they die anyway. In not being successful, you're prolonging the agony for birds and animals that will die anyway."

— Alaskan biologist Cal Lensink, speaking about the wildlife rescue efforts.

over a slick. Dispersants make oil slicks break up into tiny droplets. Dispersants don't remove oil from the water, but they keep it from forming the tarry mousse that fouls beaches, killing birds and shellfish.

Once again, officials were not prepared for the disaster. Alyeska had very little dispersant stored at Valdez. What's more, they had no equipment or aircraft to apply the chemicals to the slick. Exxon hired a private company to drop dispersants from a helicopter, but the chemicals did not mix well with the oil, and failed to work. It seemed there was nothing to stop the spill from washing up on the beaches of Prince William Sound.

Cleaning the Beaches

Once the oil hit the beaches, Exxon crews were faced with more problems. The slick had to be cleared from the sands and rocks if any wildlife in the area were to survive. The problem was how to clean the tons of tarry debris from this delicate ecosystem without causing even more damage.

At first, cleanup crews tried to wipe up the oil by hand. They gently cleaned the rocks one at a time. The process was excruciatingly slow, and it was becoming clear that hundreds of miles of shoreline would need cleaning. Exxon dropped the hand-wiping scheme after the first day.

The crews resorted to washing the

An Exxon worker scrubs an oil-covered boulder on Naked Island. Exxon stopped using this cleanup method after the first day.

fouled beaches with hot water shot from pressure hoses. The technique was fairly good at breaking up the oily sludge and forcing it back out to sea. In the first year of cleanup, 150 miles (241 km) of shoreline were cleaned with hot water. But scientists soon learned that the water — often heated to 160 degrees Fahrenheit (71 degrees Celsius) — was "cooking" the sea creatures it was meant to save.

After the first year of cleanup, Exxon used heavy lifting equipment — such as backhoes and tractors — to scoop up tar patches and to break up pools of buried oil. Tons of contaminated sand and debris were hauled away for storage or treatment.

Exxon also tried a new technique — called bioremediation — to help break down oil on the Alaskan coast. This method is based on the fact that some kinds of bacteria eat oil. Many kinds of oil-eating bacteria lived along the shores of Prince William Sound. Cleanup experts thought that applying a fertilizer to the shores would encourage the growth of these bacteria, helping them to break down the oil even faster.

Some critics of bioremediation claimed that there was no proof the fertilizer scheme would work. Others worried about the effect the fertilizers would have on the delicate ecosystem of the Sound. But the U.S. Environmental

More than one hundred eighty workers used high pressure hoses to clean the beach at Green Island.

A week after the oil spill, Dr. Jessica Porter cleans the oil off a seabird at an animal rescue center in Valdez, Alaska.

Protection Agency approved the plan. In July 1989, Exxon began to put fertilizers on hundreds of miles of shoreline. Some experts later said that the fertilizers made the oil break down at least twice as fast.

The Race to Save Wildlife

While some workers tried to clean the beaches, others worked frantically to save the birds and mammals whose lives were at risk. Thousands of dead animals already floated in the oily tide that lapped the beaches of the Sound. Here and there, some fought for life.

Scores of animal rescue workers, including many veterinarians, rushed to the scene. Some were paid by Exxon, but many came as volunteers. They set up animal rescue stations in Valdez and in the nearby towns of Cordova and Seward. Other rescuers wandered the beaches looking for survivors. Many worked for days without a break.

Saving these animals was not easy. First they had to be caught. Humans naturally frighten wild animals, so the unfortunate creatures did not realize the people were there to help. Many birds and mammals were injured as rescue workers tried to catch and hold them. Workers were often bitten and kicked. Animals that were successfully captured were sent to one of the rescue centers.

Once at the centers, many animals received treatment for low body temperature. The oil had made their feathers or fur sticky so they couldn't stay warm. Many animals had gone for days without eating or drinking, and they needed food and water. Then the animals were cleaned.

Rescue workers had to work fast to save the animals. They wanted to get them back to the wild before the stress of capture and diseases from being

Steller sea lions perch on oily rocks after the spill.

An oil spill makes birds' feathers sticky. They cannot stay warm in Alaska's frigid waters and cold March air.

touched by humans affected them. But the process of washing oil away took time. And many places where the animals lived remained contaminated with oil.

It took hours to clean birds such as gulls and ducks. A rescue worker gently scrubbed the bird's features with a toothbrush. The workers found that Dawn® dishwashing soap worked best because it cut through the oil and was gentle on the bird's skin. The makers of Dawn® donated hundreds of gallons of it to the rescue effort.

To wash around the eyes, workers used Water Piks®, which were actually designed to help humans clean their teeth. These devices shoot a small stream of water that could remove the oil without hurting the bird's eyes. Each bird was then rinsed many times and then dried before being released. In all, the International Bird Rescue Research Center cared for more than sixteen hundred seabirds in six months.

Another rescue center treated hundred of sea otters. Clumps of oil

"Like Chocolate Pudding"

"When we first got here, it was just like wading through chocolate pudding. The birds were unrecognizable. We had to have tons of kerosene to wash ourselves off."

— Cleanup worker Jeff Johnson

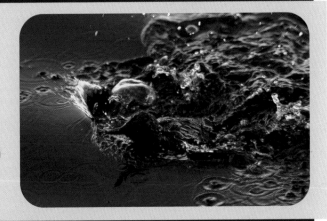

matted the otters' thick coats and damaged their lungs, stomachs, and livers. Workers treated the otters for oil poisoning and carefully washed each one. It often took several workers hours to clean just one otter. The cost of saving one otter came to about $80,000.

In all, the otter rescue centers treated more than 350 animals and saved 226 of them. Many adult otters were too sick to be released. They were sent to seaquariums for more care. Thirteen otter pups born in the rescue center were kept in captivity until they were old enough to take care of themselves.

Human Suffering

For the humans who lived on the Sound, the spill was not deadly. But it had a terrible impact on them all the same. Hardest hit were the twenty-two hundred Native villagers who lived on the coast. These people relied on the waters of the Sound for the food they ate. They made their own clothing from the skins of sea mammals. Most villagers

A rescue worker on Kodiak Island, Alaska, about 300 miles (483 km) southwest of Prince William Sound, carries a bald eagle carcass. The bird was tested to see if it died because of the Exxon Valdez oil spill.

had no jobs and little money. The sea took care of them, just as it had their parents, grandparents, and great-grandparents for centuries.

The *Exxon Valdez* spill turned the lives of these Native people upside down. The fish, shellfish, and seabirds they counted on were dying before their eyes. The water they lived on stank with oil. The smell was so strong it got into their houses, right through the walls. The state government closed their hunting and fishing areas for fear of poisoning. For many Natives, it seemed as if the world were coming to an end.

Other Native bands tried to help by sending food to the villages on Prince William Sound. Exxon also sent food. But it made some mistakes. Salt sent to help the Natives preserve fish turned out to be road salt, used for melting ice. Exxon also sent a barge of crab and shrimp. but people who ate the shellfish got sick. They found out the crab and shrimp were not fit for humans to eat. They were meant for sick otters instead.

This Native woman who was crying over death caused by the oil spill was told, "Cry for one and try to save the rest."

The Natives were angry. They thought they were being treated like animals.

Commercial fishermen in the area also suffered from the spill. To head off poisoning and to protect fish populations damaged by the oil, the state did not allow fishermen to catch herring. The state also limited the salmon catch. Before the spill, fishermen were catching huge amounts of herring and salmon. Many had spent a lot of money to buy bigger boats and more equipment. They were counting on a big catch in 1989. Instead, fishermen were told they could not fish at all. In the spring and summer after the spill, fishermen lost more than $136 million. Also, many of the tourist attractions in the area were shut down because of the oil spill.

Throughout the nation, people were stunned. Ever since Alaska became a state, many Americans liked to think of

"No First Fish"

"We walked the beaches, but the snails and the barnacles and the chitons are falling off the rocks, dead. We caught our first fish, the annual first fish, the traditional delight of all; but it got sent to the state to be tested for oil. No first fish this year."

— Chief Walter Meganack,
Alaskan Native

Hats with netting protect Alaskan fishermen from insects as they pull aboard a purse-seine net full of salmon. This type of net is stretched out in the water between two boats around a school of fish. Then the boats circle to meet each other, bringing the ends of the net together. The final step is to close the bottom of the net and get the fish.

Fears regarding the edibility of fish caught in Prince William Sound after the *Exxon Valdez* spill idled scores of commercial fishing vessels in nearby Cordova, Alaska.

A brown bear smeared with oil runs along an oil-fouled beach in Katmai National Park, Alaska.

it as one of the nation's last clean, wild places. Now televised news reports showed pictures of oil-stained beaches and dead seals and otters floating in greasy black pools. People were angry. They demanded to know who was responsible. Their attention focused on Exxon and on Captain Hazelwood. People demanded harsh punishments for both.

Even though the spill was far from the world's largest, the fact that it happened in Alaska alarmed people all over the globe. World oil prices shot to record levels. Environmentalists called for an end to oil drilling in sensitive ecosystems. They also called for tighter controls on oil tankers.

By the end of the first cleanup season, it was clear that the *Exxon Valdez* spill was a huge disaster.

Experts estimated that about a quarter of a million seabirds were directly killed by the slick or died later from eating poisoned fish. More than three thousand sea otters died — one out of every three otters that lived in the Sound. The spill also killed 300 harbor seals, 250 bald eagles, and as many as 22 killer whales. Native villages and local economies were devastated.

It was clear the oil-spill nightmare was not over.

Chapter 4

"A Part of Us is **Missing**"

The cleanup of Prince William Sound lasted three years. Every spring as the ice cleared and the snows began to thaw, thousands of workers returned to the area. Hotels crammed with workers. Many out-of-work fishermen found jobs with the cleanup crews as well. Locals referred to the hundreds of ships and aircraft that circled the Sound as "Exxon's Navy."

Crews went on washing beaches, hauling oily sand, and spraying fertilizer until 1991. Most experts believe that the natural action of waves in the Sound

An acronym poem from a student at Mount Eccles Elementary School in Valdez, Alaska, reflects the child's feelings about the oil spill.

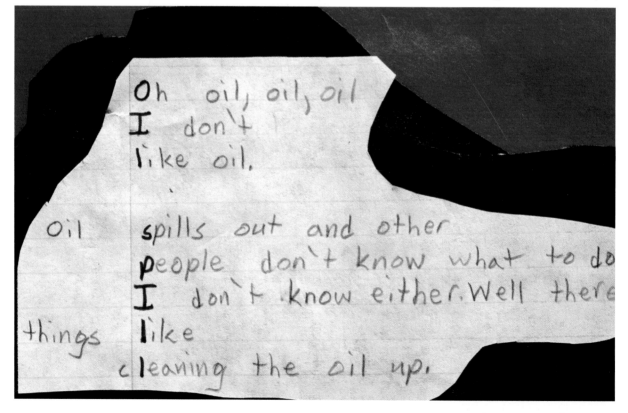

Oh oil, oil, oil
I don't
like oil.

Oil spills out and other
people don't know what to do
I don't know either. Well there
things like
cleaning the oil up.

Cleanup crews on oil-soaked Naked Island in Prince William Sound became covered in oil themselves.

cleaned off more oil than any of the human efforts. By 1992, experts thought less than a mile (1.6 km) of beach was still heavily oiled. But small pockets of oil were discovered for years afterwards. A U.S. government survey in 2001 showed that 20 acres (8 hectares) of shoreline in the Sound were still contaminated with small amounts of oil. The researchers warned that the oil is affecting the animals.

Many kinds of animals fought their way back to recovery. Bald eagles and salmon are back to their pre-spill numbers. Sea otters are making a comeback, too, but there are still fewer of them than before the spill. Killer whales are growing in numbers. The deaths in their family groups — or pods — did not cause them to split up, as some scientists had feared.

Five years after the oil spill, researchers investigated the impact of the disaster. Here they examine fucus, an important seaweed. Their research suggested that oil cleanup efforts harmed fucus and other seaweeds. Based in part on their reports, the National Oceanic and Atmospheric Administration (NOAA) said that the oil cleanup did more harm than good.

Where's the *Exxon Valdez* Now?

After the accident, tugboats towed the *Exxon Valdez* from Bligh Reef to a nearby island. There, divers patched the rips in the hull. Three months later, other tugs hauled the *Exxon Valdez* to San Diego, California, for permanent repairs and further renovations.

Today, the *Exxon Valdez* sails under the name *SeaRiver Mediterranean*. The ship is still used to carry oil. Federal law prohibits the *S/R Mediterranean* from ever entering Prince William Sound again.

Tugboats escort the rechristened *Exxon Mediterranean* from the National Steel and Shipbuilding Company's shipyard in San Diego Bay on July 20, 1990. The ship was renamed the *SeaRiver Mediterranean* in 1993. It now carries crude oil between the Middle East and Europe.

For other kinds of animals, the news is not so good. Nearly fifteen years after the accident, harbor seals were as scarce as they were just after the spill. Herring, which so many other animals depend on for food, have not recovered from the accident, either. Populations of loons, cormorants, and other waterbirds remain low. Some environmentalists fear these species may be permanent victims of the *Exxon Valdez* spill.

Life for the human residents of Prince William Sound is also returning to normal. Fisherman suffered for years after the spill as fish populations slowly recovered. After a good season the year before the spill, the salmon catch dropped to its lowest point in fifteen years. Even as late as 2000, fishermen were still not earning as much as they were in the years before the disaster.

Native Alaskan villagers say that the water is not fully back to life. The clams, mussels, and seals they rely on have not fully recovered. For the Native peoples, this means more than just a loss of food. Hunting and fishing, cooking and sharing food had all been part of the customs and traditions that made them a community.

With fishing and hunting falling off, many felt their native way of life was fading. Fewer young people were learning the Native ways. People were less willing to share the food they caught. Older people in the villages, who had always been valued for their knowledge of traditional ways, were not listened to as much. As one Native in Cordova said of the loss of their old ways, "Without those things, a part of us is missing."

The Case Against Exxon

People were angry about what had happened in Prince William Sound and looked for someone to blame. Many blamed Exxon. Native groups, commercial fisherman, the State of Alaska, and the U.S. government itself took the oil company to court. They wanted Exxon to pay for the damages.

Exxon executives said that what had happened was just an accident.

Joseph Hazelwood, former captain of the *Exxon Valdez*, sits in a courtroom on January 29, 1990 in Anchorage, Alaska, as his trial begins.

Spread of oil from the Exxon Valdez

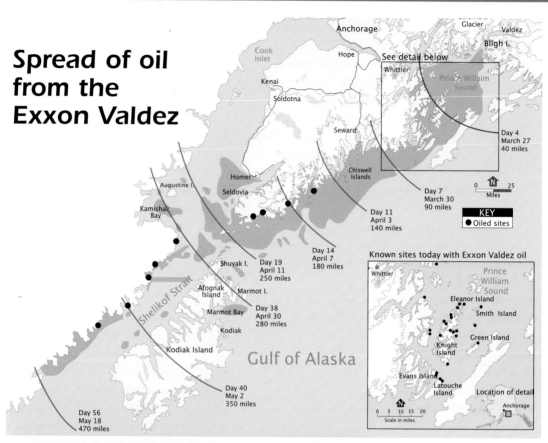

Anchorage

Glacier
Valdez
Bligh I.

Cook Inlet

Hope

See detail below

Whittier

Prince Willaim Sound

Kenai

Soldotna

Seward

Day 4
March 27
40 miles

Chiswell Islands

Augustine I.

Homer

Seldovia

Day 7
March 30
90 miles

0   N   25
Miles

Kamishak Bay

Day 11
April 3
140 miles

KEY
● Oiled sites

Shuyak I.

Day 19
April 11
250 miles

Day 14
April 7
180 miles

Known sites today with Exxon Valdez oil

Afognak Island

Marmot I.

Whittier

Prince William Sound

Sholikof Strait

Marmot Bay

Day 38
April 30
280 miles

Eleanor Island

Smith Island

Kodiak

Green Island

Kodiak Island

Knight Island

Gulf of Alaska

Evans Island

Latouche Island

Location of detail

Day 40
May 2
350 miles

0 5 10 15 20
Scale in miles

N

Anchorage

Day 56
May 18
470 miles

Anchorage Daily News graphic based on source information from the Department of Environmental Conservation.

The U.S. Coast Guard's Marine Safety office in Valdez, Alaska, tracks shipping traffic through Prince William Sound to prevent tragedies similar to that caused by the *Exxon Valdez*.

The Search For Alternatives

Since the energy crisis of the 1970s, energy companies and automakers have searched for other fuels to power cars. One option is gasohol — gasoline mixed with ethanol, or grain alcohol. Ethanol is produced from fermenting corn. Gasohol burns cleaner than gasoline, and corn is a renewable resource. So far, gasohol is even more expensive to produce than straight gasoline.

Detroit has created new cars, called hybrids, which use a combination of gasoline engines and electric motors to boost fuel efficiency to up to 60 miles (95 km) a gallon. President George W. Bush has also called for more research to produce cars that run on fuel cells. Fuel cells produce electricity through a chemical reaction that turns hydrogen gas into water. The plan calls for the first hydrogen cars to be on the market in the year 2010.

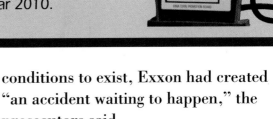

They claimed to have followed normal operating procedures and safety precautions for moving tankers in and out of the port at Valdez. The spill was a tragedy, Exxon said, but it wasn't their fault.

Prosecutors did not agree. They pointed out that Exxon had let their tanker operate with too few crew members. If there had been enough bridge officers on the *Exxon Valdez* that night, someone might have noticed the ship was off course. Overworked crews sometimes put in eighteen-hour shifts. They were often very tired and unable to pay attention to their jobs.

Even worse, Exxon managers knew Captain Hazelwood sometimes drank before driving the ship. Still, they let him operate a huge tanker in a waterway filled with risks. By allowing these

conditions to exist, Exxon had created "an accident waiting to happen," the prosecutors said .

The legal case against Exxon lasted many years as lawyers on both sides fought in court. In the end, the jury decided against Exxon. In 1991, the corporation agreed to pay more than $1 billion to the victims of the *Exxon Valdez*. The money took a long time to reach the victims.

Part of that money went to a special trust to protect land in Prince William Sound. The trust has purchased more than 500,000 acres (200,000 ha) of land in the area, keeping it safe from logging and commercial development. Scientists hope that this undeveloped area will help the Sound's wildlife thrive in their natural habitats.

Captain Joseph Hazelwood had his

own troubles in court. He was fired within days of the accident. A few weeks later, he was charged with improperly operating a vessel. The jury found him innocent of that charge but guilty of negligent release of oil. He was ordered to pay $50,000 in damages and do one thousand hours of community service. Hazelwood never worked again as a tanker captain. Instead, he got an office job with the law firm that defended him in court. He returned to Alaska for a month each summer for five years to serve his community service sentence, picking up trash from highways around the Anchorage area.

Back in Washington, D.C., Congress reacted to public anger by passing the Oil Pollution Act in 1990. The law had been proposed fourteen years earlier, but pressure from the oil industry always kept it from passing. The law made oil producers legally responsible for spills. It created a trust fund to provide money for cleanup efforts. It also required all ports that allowed oil tanker traffic to have an emergency plan ready to react quickly to spills.

Further, the Oil Pollution Act requires that by the year 2015, all oil tankers operating in U.S. waters must have an inner and an outer hull. Most oil tankers were built with a single hull — when it bursts, all the oil can escape. In a double-hull tanker, even if a collision cracks the outer hull, the inner

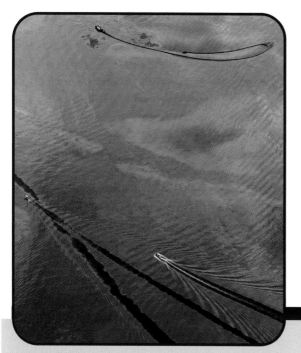

Boats wakes of clean water split the oil one day after the spill.

"Reprehensible Conduct"

"It is undisputed that Exxon understood and well knew the risks attendant to transporting crude oil out of Valdez, Alaska, and through Prince William Sound. Moreover — and these additional facts make Exxon's conduct very reprehensible — Exxon knew that . . . Captain Hazelwood was drinking and driving the crude oil tanker *Exxon Valdez* and did nothing about it."

— From a court ruling by Judge H. Russel Holland

On January 10, 2003, Spanish soldiers clean oil that washed ashore from the breakup of the *Prestige* oil tanker. The *Prestige* sank off Spain's northwest Atlantic coast on November 19, 2002.

hull could safely hold oil. Oil shippers began building the more expensive, double-hulled tankers to meet the demands of the new law. They say they are on target to meet the 2015 deadline.

Other changes have made the port of Valdez safer from oil spills. A better design for the communication systems between ships and traffic centers causes less confusion for tanker operators. Two ships now follow every tanker that goes in and out of port. One is a tugboat that helps steer the tanker if it gets into trouble. The other ship acts as a scout, watching for icebergs and reefs.

Alyeska added a huge new fleet of skimmers and recruited and trained cleanup crews to respond quickly to spills. New rules govern who can operate tankers. The Coast Guard installed a $7 million system that tracks the position of every tanker in the Sound at all times. Tankers now travel slower in bad weather. With all these new safeguards in place, the oil industry hopes the *Exxon Valdez* will be nothing but a bad memory.

But the spill lingers in the memory of many Americans. After the *Exxon Valdez* disaster, many people protested against searching for more oil in Alaska and other wild areas. In 2002, a plan to allow oil drilling in the Gulf of Mexico off the coast of Florida brought a storm of protest from the people in the area. Residents of shipping ports all over the U.S. demand tight controls on oil tankers coming in and out of their waters.

Continued accidents in the oil industry have not eased concerns about the shipping of oil. A rupture in the Trans-Alaska Pipeline System in 2001 spilled as much as 60,000 gallons (227,000 l) of crude oil onto Alaska's North Slope. And in November 2002, the tanker *Prestige* broke up off the coast of Spain, spilling about 5 million gallons (18 million l) of oil — about half the amount spilled from the *Exxon Valdez*. These and other spills prove that shipping oil is still far from safe.

Future Energy: Unanswered Questions

America's need for oil continues to grow. Ironically, many of the same people who demand tougher rules for the oil industry also drive SUVs, or Sport Utility Vehicles — some of the most popular private vehicles in the United States. SUVs are classified as trucks and do not have to live up to the fuel-efficiency laws that control the miles-per-gallon levels required for regular cars. Americans have also been slow to make their homes more fuel efficient. Demand for heating and air conditioning continues to climb as people refuse to conserve energy.

America's power hunger leads to increased pressure for new sources of oil. In 2001, President Bush proposed opening the Arctic National Wildlife Refuge (ANWR) in northern Alaska for oil drilling. People who favor the plan say the United States could extract as much as 16 billion barrels (15.5 billion British barrels) of oil from this 1.5-million-acre (607,000-ha) area of protected coastline. Critics not only question the accuracy of that estimation of the oil located in the ANWR, but also claim that drilling for it would spoil

War in Iraq — an *Exxon Valdez* legacy?

Some experts say that the slowdown of domestic oil production (that is, oil pumped from U.S. territories) that followed the *Exxon Valdez* accident made the country more dependent on imports of foreign oil, especially from Middle East countries such as Iraq. And although U.S. leaders classify Iraq as a terrorist nation, the U.S. buys about eight percent of its crude oil from Iraq. The United States waged war in Iraq twice: during Operation Desert Storm in 1991 and again in Operation Enduring Freedom in 2003.

Snow-capped mountain peaks of Montague Island rise above Prince William Sound.

another unbroken wilderness.

The argument about drilling in the ANWR continues, as does the disagreement about what the United States should do to meet its energy needs. Those who say the country needs more money to stay safe and independent disagree with those who want to protect forests and oceans from poisoning.

Meanwhile, everything is quiet once more in Prince William Sound.

Time Line

1902	First commercial discovery of oil in Alaska.
1968	Prudhoe Bay oil field discovered.
1973	Arab oil embargo creates fuel shortages in the United States.
1974	Alyeska begins building the Trans-Alaska Pipeline System.
1977	Trans-Alaska Pipeline System finished; tankers begin shipping oil through Prince William Sound.
1989	March 24: *Exxon Valdez* runs aground in Prince William Sound, dumping 11 million gallons (42 million l) of crude oil.
	March 25: Skimmers begin trying to clean up the oil.
	March 28: Oil begins washing ashore.
	March 31: Cleanup and wildlife rescue crews begin work.
	September: Wildlife rescue stations end operations.
1990	Second year of cleanup operations.
	July: Congress passes Oil Pollution Act with tougher rules for the oil industry.
1991	Third and final year of cleanup operations.
1994	June: Federal jury finds Exxon guilty of reckless operations in *Exxon Valdez* case.
2001	July: Government studies find many beaches in Prince William Sound are still contaminated with oil.

Glossary

Alyeska the partnership formed by seven major oil companies to build and operate the Trans-Alaska Pipeline System.

barrel a common unit of measurement for crude oil, equal to 42 gallons (159 liters).

bioremediation using bacteria to destroy toxic substances, especially oil.

boom a barrier that floats on the surface to trap oil. Oil floats because it is lighter than water.

bridge the command center of a ship.

crude oil the form that oil is in as it is pumped from the earth.

dispersants chemicals that break down oil into tiny droplets.

energy crisis the period from 1973 to 1974 when some Middle Eastern oil-producing countries refused to sell crude oil to the United States.

Environmental Protection Agency (EPA) the agency of the U.S. government charged with regulating pollution.

ethanol a corn-based alcohol that can be used as fuel.

enzymes proteins that cause biochemical reactions at certain temperatures.

fermenting the active process that uses enzymes to break down an energy-rich compound into its many parts.

fry recently hatched or very young fish.

hold the area on a ship that carries cargo.

Inuit (In new it) a native North American group of people who live from Alaska to Greenland; sometimes called Eskimos.

legacy a situation, circumstance, or way of thinking that gets passed down to future generations.

mousse a thick, foamy mixture formed when oil and water mix by wave action.

prosecutor a person, usually an attorney, who brings charges against another person or organization.

reef a coral or rock ridge that rises from the ocean floor to just beneath the surface of the water; a hazard to ships.

reprehensible worthy of condemnation; being at fault

scout to serve as a lookout.

skimmers special ships that scoop spilled oil from the surface of water.

supertanker an oil tanker that carries more than 200,000 tons (203,000 tonnes) of crude oil.

SUV (sports utility vehicle) a large private vehicle that does not have to follow minimum mile-per-gallon gasoline efficiency requirements.

tanker a ship designed to carry large quantities of fluids, especially oil.

thrive to experience a strong, hardy life.

toxin a poisonous substance.

For More Information

Books

The Exxon Valdez. Great Disasters: Reforms and Ramifications (series).
  Tracey E. Dils (Chelsea House)

One Wing's Gift: Rescuing Alaska's Wild Birds. Joan Harris (Alaska Northwest Books)

Sea Otter Rescue: The Aftermath of an Oil Spill. Roland Smith (Penguin Putnam)

Sludge and Slime: Oil Spills in Our World. Man-Made Disasters (series). August Greeley
  (Rosen)

What if We Run Out of Fossil Fuels? High Interest Books (series). Kimberly M. Miller
  (Scholastic)

Videos

Alaska: Spirit of the Wild. (Goldhil Home Media 2)

Black Tide: The Nightmare of Oil Spills. Twentieth Century with Mike Wallace (series).
  (A&E Entertainment)

Dead Ahead: Exxon Valdez Disaster. (Imperial Entertainment)

The Prize — The Epic Quest for Oil, Money & Power.
  (Home Vision Entertainment)

Web Sites

Environmental Protection Agency: *Exxon Valdez*
www.epa.gov/oilspill/exxon.htm

Exxon: Valdez Bulletin
www2.exxonmobil.com/Corporate/Newsroom/Publications/valdez_bulletin

Exxon Valdez Oil Spill Trustee Council — Questions and Answers
www.oilspill.state.ak.us/facts/qanda.html

NASA: Oil Pollution
seawifs.gsfc.nasa.gov/OCEAN_PLANET/HTML/peril_oil_pollution.html

National Oceanographic and Atmospheric Administration: Images from the *Exxon Valdez* Spill
response.restoration.noaa.gov/photos/exxon/exxon.html

Index

Alaska Oil Spill Commission 9, 17
Alaska Permanent Fund 12
Aleuts 12
alternative energy 9, 15, 39
Alyeska 14, 15, 16, 20, 25, 41
American settlers 12
Amoco Cadiz 15
Anchorage, Alaska 11, 14, 37, 40
Arctic National Wildlife Refuge (ANWR) 9, 42
Argo Merchant 15

bacteria 26
bald eagles 7, 30, 33, 35
bears 12, 13, 21, 33
Beaufort Sea 14
Beyon, L. R. 14
bioremediation 26
Bligh Reef 5, 6, 16, 17, 18, 19, 22, 36
booms 23, 24
Bush, President George W. 9, 39, 42

Chenega, Alaska 12
cleanup 6, 7, 20, 23, 24, 25, 26, 27, 29, 33, 34, 35,
    40, 41
Copper River 13
Cordova, Alaska 8, 9, 19, 28, 32, 37
Cousins, Gregory 18, 19,
crude oil (see oil, crude)

Dawn® dishwashing liquid 29
Diesel Beach 2
dispersants 24, 25

Environmental Protection Agency (EPA) 9, 26
energy crisis 8, 14, 15, 39
energy policy 8, 9, 39
Eskimos (see Inuits)
ethanol 39
Evandoff,Gail 12

Exxon 17, 20, 23, 24, 25, 26, 28, 31, 33, 34,
    37, 38, 39, 40
Exxon Mediterranean 36

Fairbanks, Alaska, 11
fermenting 39
fertilizers 15, 26, 28, 34
fishing 7, 10, 13, 21, 31, 32, 37
food chain 21
fry 24

glaciers 10
Greenpeace 2, 22
gold 13,
Goose Island, Alaska 6

Hazelwood, Joseph 6, 17, 18, 19, 20, 33, 37, 39, 40
herring 7, 10, 11, 31, 37
Holland, Russel H. 40

icebergs 10, 18, 41
Iditarod 11
Inuits 12
International Bird Rescue Research Center 29
Iraq 42

Johnson, Jeff 29
Juneau, Alaska 11

Katmai National Park, Alaska 33
Kenai Peninsula 14
killer whales 7, 10, 33, 35
kittiwakes 10
Knight Island, Alaska 2
Kodiak Island, Alaska, 30
Kunkel, James 20

lawsuits 37, 39, 40
legacy 42

Lensink, Cal 24
Meganack, Walter 7, 31
Middle East 9, 14, 15, 42
Middletown, Pennsylvania 8
mineral prospectors 10
Montague Island, Alaska 43
Mount Eccles Elementary School 34
mousse 21, 25
Murphy, William 17

Naked Island, Alaska 25, 35
Nantucket Island, Massachusetts 15
National Oceanic and Atmospheric Administration
    (NOAA) 35
National Steel and Shipbuilding Company 36
Native Alaskans 5, 7, 10, 12, 14, 21, 22, 30, 31,
    33, 37
Nome, Alaska 11

Oil Pollution Act of 1990 40, 41
oil
    behavior of spilled 19, 20, 21, 24, 34, 39, 40
    crude 5, 6, 40
    discovery in Alaska 13
    drilling 13
    exploration 9, 41, 42
    use 8, 9, 14, 15, 42
    impact on animals 6, 7, 17, 21, 28, 29, 30,
        31, 33
    shipping 11, 14, 15, 16, 22, 33, 40, 42
orca (see Killer Whales)
otters 7

pigeon guillemot 21
Porter, Jessica 27
Prestige 22, 41, 42
Prince William Sound, Alaska 5, 6, 11, 12, 19, 20,
    24, 25, 26, 32, 38, 43
    continued pollution in 2, 35
    oil shipping in 14, 15, 18, 40, 41
    people living on 7, 10, 11, 12, 21, 30, 31, 37
    recovery of 7, 34, 35, 36, 37, 39
    unspoiled nature of 9, 10
    wildlife in 10, 11, 12, 28, 29, 30, 33, 39

Prudhoe Bay, Alaska 12, 14

Ruel, Devan 19
Russia 13
Russians 12

salmon 7, 10, 11, 31, 32, 35, 37
scout 41
SeaRiver Mediterranean 36
sea lions 12, 28
seabirds 5, 7, 8, 29, 31, 33
seals 5, 6, 7, 10, 12, 33, 37
Seward, Alaska 28
shellfish 12
skimmers 24, 41
Spain 22, 41, 42
subsistence 12
supertankers 5, 11, 17, 18
SUV (sports utility vehicle) 42

tankers 8, 11, 14, 15, 17, 22, 33, 39, 40, 41, 42
Three Mile Island nuclear accident 8
Trans-Alaska Pipeline System (TAPS) 13, 14, 15, 42
tugboats 16, 17, 18, 36, 41

United States Coast Guard 6, 20, 38, 41
United States Congress 8, 40

Valdez, Alaska 4, 5, 11, 14, 15, 16, 20, 25, 27, 28,
    34, 38, 39, 40, 41
Valdez Vessel Traffic Center 18

Water Pik® 29
White, Tom 13
Whitman, Christine Todd 9
wildlife rescue 17, 24, 28, 29, 30